# DISCOVERING
# WHALES,
## DOLPHINS & PORPOISES

by Kelly Gauthier

Illustrated by Julius Csotonyi

APPLESAUCE PRESS

KENNEBUNKPORT, MAINE

13-Digit ISBN: 978-1-60433-961-1
10-Digit ISBN: 1-60433-961-6

This book may be ordered by mail from the publisher. Please include $5.99 for postage and handling.
Please support your local bookseller first!

Books published by Cider Mill Press Book Publishers are available at special discounts for bulk purchases in the United States by corporations, institutions, and other organizations.
For more information, please contact the publisher.

Cider Mill Press Book Publishers
"Where Good Books Are Ready for Press"
PO Box 454
12 Spring Street
Kennebunkport, Maine 04046
Visit us online! cidermillpress.com

Typography: Gipsiero, Destroy, Imperfect, PMN Caecilia
Image Credits: All illustrations by Julius Csotonyi.
All vectors used under official license from Shutterstock.com.

Printed in China
1 2 3 4 5 6 7 8 9 0
First Edition

# TABLE OF CONTENTS

# INTRODUCTION

Welcome to the underwater world of aquatic mammals! Many aquatic mammals are part of a big group of animals called cetaceans. This group includes whales, dolphins, and porpoises. Each of the three main groups has its own set of subgroups, but they all share a few common features.

Cetaceans are all mammals, just like humans, which means that they breathe air through lungs (instead of gills, like fish), are warm-blooded (instead of cold-blooded, like reptiles), they give birth to live young (instead of laying eggs, like birds), and produce milk (like cows). They may not look like it with their smooth skin, but they usually have a little bit of hair or fur at some point in their life. Some cetaceans have hair even before they are born, called lanugo. Cetaceans also have a layer of fat, called blubber, that helps them to stay warm in the chilly waters of the ocean, but they have to come up to the surface to breathe air before they can dive down again.

These aquatic mammals have adapted to life in the water. Instead of legs they have two front flippers or fins, called pectoral fins, and one long tail with features called flukes. They have blowholes on the top of their head instead of nostrils, and these blowholes help them to breathe when they reach the surface of the water. Some cetaceans have a dorsal fin (which is often a triangle shape) on their backs, but some do not.

There are two major groups of cetaceans: toothed whales (odontocetes), which includes dolphins and porpoises, and baleen whales (mysticetes).

Toothed whales, as the name suggests, have teeth. Some only have a few teeth, and some have a full set of teeth. Sometimes, these teeth are used for eating, but they are also sometimes used for protection or fighting if the whale only has a small number of teeth. Whales that do not use their teeth to eat will suction feed, which means they use powerful muscles to suck up their prey (usually fish or squid) and swallow it whole. In general, toothed whales tend to be social and live in groups called pods, and they often use a form of navigation called echolocation, in which they make noises and then use the echoes to understand their surroundings. This form of navigation is especially helpful in deep or murky water where it's difficult to see.

Instead of teeth, baleen whales have special filters in their mouths called baleen. They eat by gulping in a big mouthful of water and then using the baleen to separate the water from the food. Even though these whales are very large, they usually only eat very small animals such as krill, plankton, and small fish. They typically have two blowholes and are some of the biggest mammals in the world.

You might be wondering how whales, dolphins, and porpoises are different from one another. Although they're all part of the cetacean group, they are in separate families created by scientists because of their size, shape, and habitat.

Whales are the biggest of this group in size and can be found all over the world. They have lots of thick blubber on their bodies, which often allows them to live in very cold or very deep water.

Dolphins are typically smaller than whales and in general prefer warmer or tropical waters. Some species of dolphins can even live in freshwater. They are athletic swimmers and are often known for being able to do acrobatics and tricks.

Although porpoises are a smaller family than dolphins and whales, there are a number of different porpoise species, including some that can live in freshwater. These animals are often small in size compared to whales and some dolphins, and they usually live in cooler waters than dolphins.

Dolphins and porpoises are sometimes threatened by sharks, but most whales are large enough that they are not threatened. One of the biggest threats to cetaceans comes from people. For years, whales were hunted for their valuable blubber, driving some species to near extinction. Although smaller dolphins and porpoises were not hunted as aggressively as whales, they are often caught in the nets of fishermen—sometimes accidentally—and injured or killed. Like all ocean life, pollution and climate change are major threats to cetaceans because changes in their habitat can affect their food supply and quality of life.

# PREHISTORIC CETACEANS

You might not know it by looking at them, but hippos are the closest relative to whales, and both whales and hippos likely share a common ancestor millions of years ago. There were a lot of evolutionary steps in the history of whales, but one thing we can learn about them from their hippo relatives (and some of the other species that came before them) is that whale ancestors probably had legs and walked on land.

It might seem crazy to think of whales with legs, but these ancestors were likely able to live both on land and in the water, much like modern-day hippos do, so they would have breathed air and been able to walk and swim. Eventually, they evolved from having legs to having fins, but they kept the ability to breathe air. Their front legs eventually morphed into flippers, their tails elongated, and their back legs disappeared entirely, allowing them to maneuver in the water more efficiently. We know this because the hip bones of some modern whales show evidence that their ancestors had hind legs.

In this section, we'll look at some of the prehistoric ancestors of modern-day whales and the important traits they developed and passed on that helped them to move from land to sea, as well as some prehistoric cetaceans that looked similar to modern-day dolphins, porpoises, and whales.

# PAKICETUS
## PAKICETUS INACHUS

**WHEN:** About 56 to 40 million years ago
**WHERE:** Modern Pakistan
**SIZE:** 100 pounds (45 kg), roughly the size of a wolf
**LOOK FOR:** A rodentlike animal with a long tail and a long snout
**PREHISTORIC PROFILE:** *Pakicetus* looks like a land animal, but it has a lot more in common with modern whales and hippos than you might think. *Pakicetus* had an ear bone that was similar to the unique ear bone in modern whales, as well as an anklebone associated with hoofed animals, making it possible that *Pakicetus* was a distant ancestor to both whales and hippos. This carnivorous, four-legged animal is thought to have eaten both meat and fish, which makes it likely that it was able to navigate both land and sea.

# AMBULOCETUS
## AMBULOCETUS NATANS

**WHEN:** About 49 million years ago
**WHERE:** Modern Pakistan
**LENGTH:** 9¾ feet (3 meters)
**LOOK FOR:** Webbed feet and a long snout full of teeth.
**PREHISTORIC PROFILE:** It's not hard to picture *Ambulocetus* in the water with its crocodile-like snout. Although *Ambulocetus* still had legs, its feet had flipper-like qualities to them, including webbed hind feet. To move around on land, this heavy creature may have waddled or used its front legs to pull it along similar to how modern sea lions move.

Studies of *Ambulocetus* skulls helped scientists to understand that this creature was likely able to swallow food underwater, and it had teeth that were similar in shape to other cetacean ancestors. By studying the chemicals in their teeth, scientists were able to discover that they likely fed in both freshwater and saltwater.

# PROTOCETUS
## PROTOCETUS ATAVUS

**WHEN:** 48.6 to 40.4 million years ago
**WHERE:** Modern Egypt
**LENGTH:** About 8 feet (2½ meters)
**LOOK FOR:** Beak-like snout, front flippers with webbed toes, small back flippers, and a back ridge
**PREHISTORIC PROFILE:** *Protocetus atavus* means "first whale," an accurate title for this early cetacean. With a streamlined, whalelike body and a fluke tail, *Protocetus* shares many attributes found in modern day whales. *Protocetus* was discovered near modern-day Cairo, Egypt, with the first description of this early cetacean completed in 1904.

Have you ever tried listening to something underwater? Scientists believe that *Protocetus* had a set of ears that could hear underwater, as well as a good sense of smell, but unlike many modern whales they were unable to echolocate.

# BASILOSAURUS

## *BASILOSAURUS ISIS*

**WHEN:** About 37 million years ago
**WHERE:** Modern Egypt, Jordan, and Morocco
**LENGTH:** 59 to 65½ feet (18 to 20 meters)
**LOOK FOR:** An incredibly long tail compared to the rest of its body
**PREHISTORIC PROFILE:** You definitely wouldn't want to encounter a *Basilosaurus* in the ancient ocean. Scientists think *Basilosaurus* was likely a predator, and its jaws and teeth had a very powerful bite. Evidence shows that they fed on fish and sharks, and *Basilosaurus* bite marks on fossil *Dorudon atrox* skulls suggest that *Dorudon* may also have been prey to *Basilosaurus*. These massive animals may have been some of the first fully aquatic mammals. There are two different species of *Basilosaurus*, and numerous fossils found across northern Africa suggest that it likely lived during the late Eocene period.

# CORONODON

## *CORONODON HAVENSTEINI*

**WHEN:** About 30 million years ago
**WHERE:** Modern Charleston, South Carolina
**LENGTH:** 16 feet (5 meters)
**LOOK FOR:** Large, whalelike creature with a wide nose and teeth with fanlike edges
**PREHISTORIC PROFILE:** *Coronodon havensteini* used its teeth for both catching prey and filtering food out of the water, making it one of the first filter-feeding whales. First discovered in 2017, *Coronodon* provides a link between ancient whales and modern baleen whales and is part of a prehistoric group of cetaceans known as archaeocetes. Have you ever run your finger along your back teeth? You'll probably feel bumps on the surface. *Coronodon* had bumps all around its teeth, which it used to filter its food out of the water. *Coronodon* likely took in a big mouthful of prey and seawater and then forced the water back out of its mouth, catching its prey in the fanlike edges of its teeth.

# AETIOCETUS

## *AETIOCETUS WELTONI*

**WHEN:** 28 to 24 million years ago
**WHERE:** Ancient eastern North Pacific Ocean
**LENGTH:** Up to 11 feet (3.5 meters)
**LOOK FOR:** Wide, triangular, flat snout, with both baleen and teeth present
**PREHISTORIC PROFILE:** Although today we divide whales up based on whether they have teeth or baleen, *Aetiocetus weltoni* may have had both! With a jaw structure that may have allowed this ancient cetacean to expand its jaw sideways like modern baleen whales, *Aetiocetus* most likely fed on fish by trapping them in their mouth and then pushing the additional water back out. Although scientists aren't sure if the presence of early baleen made this cetacean a true filter feeder, the baleen might have helped hold on to slippery fish!

# WAHAROA
## WAHAROA RUWHENUA

**WHEN:** 27.3 to 25.2 million years ago
**WHERE:** Modern South Island of New Zealand
**LENGTH:** 16½ to 19½ feet (5 to 6 meters)
**LOOK FOR:** Long, thin mouth that opens past the eyes with teeth at the end of each jaw
**PREHISTORIC PROFILE:** Hey *Waharoa ruwhenua*, why the long face? Scientists think that these early cetaceans probably weren't lunging predators, but rather filtered their food out of the water, making them one of the early relatives of modern baleen whales. Because their jaws were very long and thin, they were also delicate, and there is evidence that their jaws did not get incredibly long until adulthood as scientists have found multiple fossils for this species at all different ages. Because of their incredibly large jaw, they were given the Māori name *waharoa*, which both means "gateway" and is the name of the horse mussel, a mussel with a long, thin, wedge-shaped shell that looks similar to *Waharoa*'s jaw.

# SWORD-SNOUTED DOLPHIN
## EURHINODELPHIS LONGIROSTRIS

**WHEN:** About 23 to 5 million years ago
**WHERE:** Modern Belgium, France, and Maryland
**LENGTH:** 6½ feet (2 meters)
**LOOK FOR:** A long, thin snout
**PREHISTORIC PROFILE:** Think about a swordfish with its long, pointed snout. The sword-snouted dolphin had a very similar (and sharp!) nose that it probably used to hunt prey. Fossils of this prehistoric cetacean have been found in Europe and the United States, and these sword-snouted dolphins lived during the Miocene period. They had complex ear bones that scientists believe may have been used for a form of echolocation.

# PHOBERODON
## *PHOBERODON ARCTIROSTRIS*

**WHEN:** 23 to 15.97 million years ago
**WHERE:** Modern Patagonia, Argentina
**LENGTH:** 10¼ feet (3 meters)
**LOOK FOR:** Sharklike teeth and a small dorsal fin
**PREHISTORIC PROFILE:** Look out, a shark! Or, well, shark-toothed dolphin. Unlike modern-day dolphins with their conical teeth, *Phoberodon arctirostris* had ridged teeth similar to modern sharks, and were part of a family of ancient cetaceans called Squalodontidae. First discovered in 1840, *Phoberodon* was not largely studied until more than 100 years later! Although most modern dolphins are not directly related to *Phoberodon*, they provide an important link to help scientists better understand how different cetaceans evolved to adapt to their environment.

# GIANT-TOOTHED SPERM WHALE
## *LIVYATAN MELVILLEI*

**WHEN:** About 13 to 12 million years ago
**WHERE:** Modern Peru
**LENGTH:** Estimated 42½ to 52½ feet (13 to 16 meters)
**LOOK FOR:** An incredibly long skull with large, piercing teeth.
**PREHISTORIC PROFILE:** When this species was first discovered, scientists wanted to name it "Leviathan," because the ancient whale had a massive skull and jaw, but that name was already taken by a species of mastodon! Instead, they named it "Livyatan." This ancient sperm whale likely lived during the Miocene era, and fossils found in Peru suggest it lived in the Pacific Ocean. Much like modern sperm whales (see page 64), *Livyatan* had a large bulge on its skull that was likely a spermaceti organ. The second part of this whale's name, *melvillei*, is actually a reference to the writer Herman Melville, who created the famous sperm whale Moby Dick. *Livyatan* teeth are truly massive, and they measure about 14 inches (35½ centimeters) long and 4 or 5 inches (10 to 13 centimeters) wide with sharp tips. For comparison, *Tyrannosaurus rex* teeth were about 6 to 12 inches (15 to 30 centimeters) long.

# WHALERUS
## ODOBENOCETOPS LEPTODON

**WHEN:** About 7 to 5 million years ago
**WHERE:** Modern Peru and Chile
**AVERAGE TUSK SIZE:** 3 feet (1 meter) on the right side, and 10 inches (25 centimeters) on the left.
**LOOK FOR:** A wide head similar to modern-day walruses with one long tusk.
**PREHISTORIC PROFILE:** What do you get when you cross a whale and a walrus? A whalerus! This extinct form of a toothed whale had a face similar in shape to a walrus and large, tusklike teeth. Because this whale had a walrus-like head and tusks, it was nicknamed the "whalerus," or "walrus whale." Their two tusks were not the same size, which makes them different from any modern marine mammals, although they are somewhat similar to modern narwhals.

# SKIMMING PORPOISE
## SEMIROSTRUM CERUTTII

**WHEN:** About 5 to 1.6 million years ago
**WHERE:** Modern California
**JAW LENGTH:** About 2¾-foot (85-centimeter) jaw
**LOOK FOR:** A long lower jaw with a comparatively short, triangular upper jaw
**PREHISTORIC PROFILE:** Imagine what it would feel like if your bottom jaw was twice as long as your upper jaw. The skimming porpoise, a prehistoric porpoise that may be related to modern porpoises, had a very interesting mouth, with a lower jaw that extended out far beyond the upper jaw. Scientists think they may have used this jaw to help them skim food from the seafloor.

# MYSTERIOUS MYSTICETES

The mysticetes group of whales (also known as baleen whales) are toothless. Instead of teeth, this type of whale has special filters in its mouth called baleen plates. To eat, baleen whales find an area of water with a big group of prey available (usually small sea crustaceans called krill). Then they take in a huge mouthful of water, pulling in both water and prey. Then they use the baleen to filter the water out of their mouth, leaving just the prey behind for the whale to swallow. Baleen whales are incredibly large, but despite their size, they're able to move around well and are even known for being able to jump entirely out of the water.

# PYGMY RIGHT WHALE

## CAPEREA MARGINATA

WHERE: Southern Hemisphere, surrounding Antarctica

LENGTH: 19¾ feet (6 meters)

DESCRIPTION: A dark and light gray whale with lighter patches behind the eyes

WHALE WATCH: Pygmy right whales earned their nickname by being the smallest of the baleen whales. These whales are distinguished from other right whales because they have a dorsal fin. These petite whales are only found in a small area near Antarctica where the water is very cold. Because they only live in this area, they're not often spotted at sea. In fact, there have only ever been about 20 recorded sightings of groups of pygmy right whales at sea, which is why we know relatively little about what they're like. Some scientists even speculate they are the last living members of an ancient type of baleen whale known as cetotheres, meaning they might not be part of the right whale family at all!

# SOUTHERN RIGHT WHALE

## *EUBALAENA AUSTRALIS*

**WHERE:** Southern Hemisphere
**LENGTH:** 49 to 59 feet (15 to 18 meters)
**LOOK FOR:** Callosities on the head and a long mouth that begins at the eye
**WHALE WATCH:** Have you ever gone sailing? Southern right whales love to go sailing by sticking their tail out of the water to catch the wind. This is called "tail sailing." Scientists aren't sure exactly why they do it, but they think it could be a way to cool off, or even a form of playing.

The Eubalaena genus has three different species of right whales and they all have white patches of rough skin on their head called callosities. There are around 13,000 southern right whales, and you can only find them in the oceans of the Southern Hemisphere. Southern right whales have been known to swim around ships and at the surface of the water.

# ANTARCTIC MINKE WHALE

## BALAENOPTERA BONAERENSIS

**WHERE:** Southern Hemisphere, surrounding Antarctica

**LENGTH:** 26¼ to 32¾ feet (8 to 10 meters)

**LOOK FOR:** Pale, thin streaks leading back from the blowhole slits

**WHALE WATCH:** You may not find people swimming in the freezing waters of Antarctica, but you'll find plenty of minke whales! These small, cold-loving whales are most often found around the edges of large masses of ice called pack ice, and minke whales are usually seen alone or in small groups. If you're ever sitting on a boat in Antarctic waters, you might even get to see one up close if you're willing to wait. Although they don't like moving boats very much, curious minke whales are known to approach stationary boats.

# OMURA'S WHALE

## BALAENOPTERA OMURAI

**WHERE:** Indian Ocean, southern Atlantic Ocean, and western Pacific Ocean
**LENGTH:** 32¾ feet (10 meters)
**LOOK FOR:** A white blaze along the back and a dark eye stripe
**WHALE WATCH:** Omura's whales (far left) are truly one of the most mysterious mysticetes. They are very rare to spot in the wild, so we don't know very much about them, and scientists suspect that they may live in a much larger area than we know about. Omura's whales are small whales that are closely related to Bryde's whales (see facing page). When they have been seen, Omura's whales are most often found in shallow shelf water rather than deep, open ocean waters, and they seem to prefer warmer, tropical waters.

# BRYDE'S WHALE

## BALAENOPTERA BRYDEI

**WHERE:** Southern Hemisphere
**LENGTH:** 49¾ feet (15 meters)
**LOOK FOR:** A long, slender whale with up to 70 expandable "throat pleats"
**WHALE WATCH:** Can you imagine being caught in the jaws of a massive whale? Rainer Schimpf can, because in March 2019, that's exactly what happened when he was caught in the path of a Bryde's whale feeding on sardines. When they're feeding, Bryde's whales will dive in a lunging motion, twisting on the way to their prey. This motion can be pretty intense, especially because these whales are so large, and the whale caught Schimpf's whole upper body in its mouth. Don't worry, it quickly spit Schimpf out unharmed, and he was lucky enough to have a nearby coworker catch it all on camera!

Unlike other baleen whales, Bryde's whales don't make big migrations with the change of seasons. Instead, they're found year-round near the equator of the Southern Hemisphere, where the waters are the warmest.

# COMMON MINKE WHALE

## BALAENOPTERA ACUTOROSTRATA

**WHERE:** Global

**LENGTH:** 32¾ feet (10 meters)

**LOOK FOR:** A large, white spot on the pectoral fins

**WHALE WATCH:** Have you heard of DNA tests that can help you learn your ancestry? The common minke whale and the Antarctic minke whale (see page 19) used to be considered the same species, but DNA testing proved that they were actually two different types of whales. Common minke whales have been seen in every ocean of the world, and generally prefer cooler waters over tropical areas. Common minke whales are most often seen alone, and they tend to stay pretty close to land—they'll even enter bays, lagoons, or estuaries!

*Minke whales are very fast swimmers, and they've been spotted jumping out of the water with acrobatic moves similar to some dolphins. The smaller whale below is a dwarf minke whale, a subspecies that has yet to be classified.*

# RIVER DWELLERS

When you think of dolphins, you might assume they live in the ocean, but some species of dolphins can live in the freshwater rivers of Asia and South America. Some dolphins are able to live in both freshwater and saltwater, which means that they can also live in estuaries (where rivers meet the ocean), or even in the ocean along the coast. Unlike ocean-dwelling dolphins, river dolphins are often smaller and have had to adapt to living in warm, shallow water. Many river dolphins are threatened species because boat travel, dams, fishing nets, and pollution destroy their habitats.

## LA PLATA DOLPHIN

### PONTOPORIA BLAINVILLEI

**WHERE:** South America
**LENGTH:** 5¾ feet (1¾ meters)
**LOOK FOR:** A small head and long, slender beak
**DOLPHIN DATA:** Did you know there's such a thing as ghost dolphin? The La Plata dolphin turns from gray-brown to white as it ages and can live for up to 20 years, causing fishermen to nickname it the "white ghost." Although La Plata dolphins can live in either freshwater or saltwater, they prefer to live along ocean coasts or in estuaries rather than just in rivers. These dolphins often feed in groups during high tide, and they have a unique hunting method where they circle around a school of fish as a group to catch them.

# IRRAWADDY DOLPHIN
## *ORCAELLA BREVIROSTRIS*

**WHERE:** Indian Ocean, Pacific Ocean, Ganges River, Mekong River, and Irrawaddy River

**LENGTH:** 6½ to 9 feet (2 to 2¾ meters)

**LOOK FOR:** Blunt, rounded face and a U-shaped blowhole

**DOLPHIN DATA:** If you've ever gone fishing you know how long you have to wait for a bite, but on the Irrawaddy River, all you need is a dolphin to help speed up your fishing success. Fishermen on the Irrawaddy River historically said that they would tap a wooden key called a "lahai kway" against the side of their boat to communicate with the Irrawaddy dolphins. The dolphins would help guide nearby schools of fish into the fishermen's nets, and in return the fishermen would share some of their catch with the dolphins.

*The Irrawaddy dolphin was named for the Irrawaddy River, where a group of these dolphins live, but Irrawaddy dolphins live in both saltwater and freshwater. In fact, this type of dolphin is more often found living along ocean coasts and in estuaries.*

# AMAZON RIVER DOLPHIN
## INIA GEOFFRENSIS

**WHERE:** South America
**LENGTH:** 7⅓ feet (2¼ meters)
**LOOK FOR:** Solid pink or mottled gray and pink
**DOLPHIN DATA:** Imagine canoeing down a river when a dolphin suddenly grabs your paddle! Amazon River dolphins, also called botos, are playful dolphins that have been seen rolling and waving their flippers, and they've even been known to bump up against canoes or grab hold of paddles. The largest of the river dolphins, male Amazon River dolphins often grow larger than the females, up to 8 feet (2½ meters) long.

Amazon River dolphins do not have a large dorsal fin like some other dolphins, but have a very flexible neck that allows them to look side to side. They can paddle one flipper forward while the other flipper paddles backward, which helps them navigate over tricky areas of the river.

# TUCUXI
## SOTALIA FLUVIATILIS

**WHERE:** South America
**LENGTH:** 5 feet (1½ meters)
**LOOK FOR:** Similar to a bottlenose dolphin (see page 45) in color, but smaller
**DOLPHIN DATA:** Tucuxi are the synchronized swimmers of the dolphin world. Although they're slow swimmers in comparison to other dolphins, tucuxi are very athletic and can do impressive stunts like flips and rolls in unison with their fellow dolphins. Tucuxi are freshwater dolphins found in areas of the Amazon and Orinoco Rivers, where they feed on fish, squid, and octopus. They're social dolphins, and are often seen swimming in pods, but they're not very fond of human interaction and will shy away from people.

# GUIANA DOLPHIN
## SOTALIA GUIANENSIS

**WHERE:** South America and Central America

**LENGTH:** 6½ (2 meters)

**LOOK FOR:** A small, gray body similar to a bottlenose dolphin (see page 45)

**DOLPHIN DATA:** Don't expect the Guiana dolphin to swim up to you like other river dolphins will. You might spot Guiana dolphins swimming in waves or jumping out of the water, but these shy dolphins usually stay away from people. The Guiana dolphin is sometimes known as the estuarine dolphin because it can live in both freshwater and saltwater, and is often found in shallow estuaries where rivers meet the ocean. The Guiana dolphin is very similar to the tucuxi dolphin (far left), but the two are considered different species because Guiana dolphins are larger than the tucuxi in both length and weight. These dolphins are usually bluish gray in color and will eat fish, squid, and crabs.

# TUXEDOS OF THE SEA

These beautiful whales, dolphins, and porpoises have put on their best attire. With intricate black-and-white markings, many of the animals in this chapter look like they have on fine tuxedos. These interesting color patterns are fun to look at, but they also help scientists to distinguish between different species when they're observing marine wildlife.

# NORTHERN RIGHT WHALE DOLPHIN

## *LISSODELPHIS BOREALIS*

**WHERE:** North Pacific Ocean

**LENGTH:** 6½ to 9¾ feet (2 to 3 meters)

**LOOK FOR:** Black body with a long, slender white patch on the underside and snout

**DOLPHIN DATA:** While their name might feel like a mouthful, it actually tells you a lot about these dolphins. Northern right whale dolphins only live in the cold, deep waters of the Pacific Ocean in the Northern Hemisphere. They also don't have a dorsal fin, like right whales, which is why they're called right whale dolphins.

# STRAP-TOOTHED WHALE

## *MESOPLODON LAYARDII*

**WHERE:** Southern Hemisphere, especially cold water
**LENGTH:** 16½ to 19¾ feet (5 to 6 meters)
**LOOK FOR:** Large, tusklike teeth growing from the lower jaw in males
**WHALE WATCH:** The male strap-toothed whale has a strange set of teeth that gave this species its nickname. The teeth grow up out of the whale's bottom jaw toward the top jaw at a sharp angle, and can grow to be up to a foot long! Despite their odd teeth, which can almost force their mouths closed, these whales feed on squid and fish.

# SOUTHERN RIGHT WHALE DOLPHIN

## *LISSODELPHIS PERONII*

**WHERE:** Southern Hemisphere, especially around the Antarctic
**LENGTH:** 6½ to 9¾ feet (2 to 3 meters)
**LOOK FOR:** White underbody and snout with a curved black patch on the top running down to the tail
**DOLPHIN DATA:** In the north you have northern right whale dolphins (see page 27), and in the south you have southern right whale dolphins. Although closely related to northern right whale dolphins, southern right whale dolphins are only found in the cold, open waters of the Southern Hemisphere. These fast-swimming dolphins sometimes perform tricks like leaps and belly flops while they swim.

# SPOTS, STRIPES & SNOOTS

There are many different types of dolphins, and the species can be classified based on location or appearance. They can have special markings, like the Atlantic spotted dolphin (see page 44) that make them unique. Or, they can be found only in specific areas, like the Burrunan dolphin (see page 42). Some dolphins are different because of the shape of their dorsal fin, like the Indian Ocean humpback dolphin (see page 41). Some are even separated by the length and shape of their beak, like the common bottlenose dolphin (see page 45) or the short-beaked common dolphin (see page 36). Technically, dolphins are all marine mammals who breathe air and swim underwater for lengths of time, but their unique features help us to differentiate between them.

## STRIPED DOLPHIN
### STENELLA COERULEOALBA

**WHERE:** Tropical oceans around the world
**LENGTH:** 8 feet (2½ meters)
**LOOK FOR:** Dark gray stripes from above the snout, over the eye, and to the underside of the body
**DOLPHIN DATA:** Striped dolphins have a unique acrobatic move called "roto-tailing," where they leap in the air and quickly rotate their tail. These fast swimmers will quickly streak away if frightened, but they have been known to swim alongside boats.

Striped dolphins live in large groups made up of hundreds of dolphins, and they have been known to interact with other species of dolphins. In fact, striped dolphins mated with spinner dolphins (see page 47) to create the hybrid Clymene dolphin (see page 44).

# PANTROPICAL SPOTTED DOLPHIN

## STENELLA ATTENUATA

**WHERE:** Tropical oceans around the world
**LENGTH:** 8 feet (2½ meters)
**LOOK FOR:** Slender, spotted bodies
**DOLPHIN DATA:** Do you like eating tuna fish sandwiches? Pantropical spotted dolphins love tuna, and these dolphins are often found swimming around schools of tuna. But their favorite food can be dangerous, because fishermen catch large quantities of tuna, and sometimes the dolphins are accidentally caught in their nets. Because of the danger to dolphins, a lot of fishermen have started to use more "dolphin-safe" fishing methods, but accidental catching, called "bycatch," is still a problem for this type of dolphin and many other cetaceans.

# CHILEAN DOLPHIN
## CEPHALORHYNCHUS EUTROPIA

**WHERE:** South America, especially coasts around Chile

**LENGTH:** 5¾ feet (1¾ meters)

**LOOK FOR:** Small, stocky body and short snout

**DOLPHIN DATA:** You might have guessed that Chilean dolphins live near Chile, but you might not know that they prefer shallow areas near the coast. They especially like areas with strong tides and will even travel into estuaries and rivers. These dolphins are usually found in small groups, but are known for being very shy toward people. Chilean dolphins live in the same area as Commerson's dolphins (see page 30); they can easily be identified because Commerson's dolphins have large, white markings on their bodies. Chilean dolphins are mostly gray, with a lighter patch along their bellies.

# HAVISIDE'S DOLPHIN

## CEPHALORHYNCHUS HEAVISIDII

**WHERE:** Atlantic Ocean

**LENGTH:** 5¾ feet (1¾ meters)

**LOOK FOR:** Black body with a white, curved marking on the side

**DOLPHIN DATA:** When you jump into the water, do you like to make a big splash? Haviside's dolphins are playful, fast swimmers, and they can gracefully jump straight out of the water, turn in the air, and then dive back into the water without making much of a splash at all! This dolphin is closely related to the Chilean dolphin (left) and the Commerson's dolphin (see page 30). Haviside's dolphins are often found in small pods, and they feed on fish, octopus, and squid.

# FRASER'S DOLPHIN

## LAGENODELPHIS HOSEI

**WHERE:** Pacific Ocean, Indian Ocean, and Atlantic Ocean, especially in deep water

**LENGTH:** 9 feet (2¾ meters)

**LOOK FOR:** A dark back with a white stomach and short snout

**DOLPHIN DATA:** Fraser's dolphins (bottom left) prefer to live in deep, tropical waters and feed hundreds of feet deep where sunlight can't help them to see, so they use a special form of navigation called echolocation, where they send calls out and then use the echoes from those calls to help them understand their surroundings. Fraser's dolphins usually travel in large pods of more than 100 dolphins.

*Short-beaked common dolphins (top) are active and very social. They're often found in pods, and they'll ride in waves and leap out of the water.*

# SHORT-BEAKED COMMON DOLPHIN

## DELPHINUS DELPHIS

**WHERE:** Atlantic Ocean, Pacific Ocean, Black Sea, Gulf of Mexico, Red Sea

**LENGTH:** 9 feet (2¾ meters)

**LOOK FOR:** White underside with a gray snout and upper back

**DOLPHIN DATA:** Short-beaked common dolphins (top left) have mostly black bodies and white bellies, but along their sides they have unique gray and yellow markings that form an hourglass shape. Like its name suggests, the short-beaked common dolphin is pretty common, and groups of this species are found all over the world. These dolphins prefer coastal waters, although occasionally they've been spotted in deeper waters. The only temperature of water they dislike is the cold of Arctic and Antarctic waters.

# LONG-BEAKED COMMON DOLPHIN

## DELPHINUS CAPENSIS

**WHERE:** Warm coastal waters

**LENGTH:** 9 feet (2¾ meters)

**LOOK FOR:** A long, thin snout and dark gray body with a yellow stripe on a white stomach

**DOLPHIN DATA:** Long-beaked common dolphins have tons of friends. They live in massive pods with hundreds of dolphins and will even form smaller groups within the larger one! These medium-size, long-beaked dolphins are found in many parts of the world along the coast, especially in warm, shallow water near California, South America, and Africa. They will also interact with other species of dolphins and whales.

# PEALE'S DOLPHIN
## LAGENORHYNCHUS AUSTRALIS

**WHERE:** South America

**LENGTH:** 6½ feet (2 meters)

**LOOK FOR:** Stocky body with short, slightly pointed snout

**DOLPHIN DATA:** Playful Peale's dolphins love looking at people on boats, and sometimes they will even float on their sides to get a better view! Peale's dolphins are very social and will interact with a variety of other whales and dolphins.

   With dark gray backs and white spots behind their flippers, Peale's dolphins look similar to the dusky dolphin (right), but Peale's dolphins have unique dark markings around their eyes. They prefer to live in coastal waters and are often found in entrances to channels where the water is very fast moving.

*Unlike other types of dolphins, Peale's dolphins do not use whistle sounds to communicate with one another, but they will use clicking noises.*

*Populations of the dusky dolphin have been spotted along the coast in South America, Africa, New Zealand, and Australia, where they feed on anchovies, squid, and shrimp.*

# DUSKY DOLPHIN

## LAGENORHYNCHUS OBSCURUS

**WHERE:** Southern Hemisphere

**LENGTH:** 6½ feet (2 meters)

**LOOK FOR:** A short beak and dark upper body with a gray stripe along the side and a white stomach

**DOLPHIN DATA:** Dusky dolphins are skilled acrobats. They'll often jump out of the water at the same time, and they can perform many different flips and spins. They communicate with each other using whistles and clicking sounds. Their dark gray, light gray, and white colors are similar to Pacific white-sided dolphins (see page 51); the two species are closely related.

# ATLANTIC HUMPBACK DOLPHIN
## SOUSA TEUSZII

**WHERE:** Atlantic Ocean, especially around the coast of Africa
**LENGTH:** 9 feet (2¾ meters)
**LOOK FOR:** Humped back with a small dorsal fin on top
**DOLPHIN DATA:** A hump-shaped dorsal fin gives these dolphins their name. They prefer warm, shallow coastal waters and bay areas, where they feed on fish, squid, and crustaceans. They are shy toward humans and don't usually interact with boats, but some fishermen have reported Atlantic humpback dolphins helping them by herding fish into their nets.

40

# INDIAN OCEAN HUMPBACK DOLPHIN

## SOUSA PLUMBEA

WHERE: Indian Ocean

LENGTH: 6½ to 8 feet (2 to 2½ meters)

LOOK FOR: Humped back with a small dorsal fin on top

DOLPHIN DATA: You might have noticed that people's hair turns gray as they get older, and Indian Ocean humpback dolphins turn gray as they age, too! Although they're born with light or white coloring, they develop patches of darker gray as they get older. The Indian Ocean humpback dolphin is closely related to Atlantic (left) and Australian humpback dolphins (see page 42), but they live mostly along the coast of Africa in the Indian Ocean. They prefer shallow, coastal waters. Like other humpback dolphins, they're named for the hump shape of their dorsal fins.

41

# AUSTRALIAN HUMPBACK DOLPHIN

## SOUSA SAHULENSIS

**WHERE:** Australia

**LENGTH:** 3 to 8 feet (1 to 2½ meters)

**LOOK FOR:** Strikingly dark dorsal fin with a cape-like pattern

**DOLPHIN DATA:** This dolphin may not be a superhero, but it does have a cape. The Australian humpback's dorsal fin is very dark, giving it the appearance of wearing a cape on its back. This type of humpback dolphin was named because it's only found in shallow coastal waters around Australia, and although it's very similar to Indian Ocean and Atlantic humpback dolphins (see pages 40-41), it does not have the same large hump along its dorsal fin. These shy dolphins do not often approach people, but they do travel in pods.

# BURRUNAN DOLPHIN

## TURSIOPS AUSTRALIS

**WHERE:** Australia

**LENGTH:** 7⅓ to 9 feet (2¼ to 2¾ meters)

**LOOK FOR:** White coloration with a gray stripe along the top of the body

**DOLPHIN DATA:** In the wild, the Burrunan dolphin might be mistaken for a common bottlenose dolphin (see page 45) because they were once thought to be the same species. But in 2011, the Burrunan dolphin was recognized as its own species. This small dolphin lives along the coast of Australia, where it prefers to live in estuaries and sheltered bay areas.

*Hunting food can be a lot of work, so Australian humpback dolphins (top) make the job easier by chasing fish into shallow areas so they're easy to catch.*

# INDO-PACIFIC HUMPBACK DOLPHIN

## SOUSA CHINENSIS

**WHERE:** Pacific Ocean

**LENGTH:** 6½ to 9¾ feet (2 to 3 meters)

**LOOK FOR:** Gray, white, or pink coloration

**DOLPHIN DATA:** The Indo-Pacific humpback dolphin has a very long life compared to most other dolphins. In the wild, they can live up to 40 years! Members of the humpback dolphin family, these dolphins are often found in warm, shallow, coastal waters along Southeast Asia, Australia, and New Guinea. These dolphins are generally gray, light pink, or white in color, which varies based on where they live and how old they are.

43

# ATLANTIC SPOTTED DOLPHIN
## STENELLA FRONTALIS

**WHERE:** Tropical Atlantic Ocean
**LENGTH:** 5 to 6½ feet (1½ to 2 meters)
**LOOK FOR:** Dark gray and white bodies with speckles in adults
**DOLPHIN DATA:** Although they're named for their unique speckled pattern as adults, Atlantic spotted dolphins are not born with spots. As they get older, they develop spots in unique patterns. Because the young dolphins don't have markings, it can be easy to confuse them with bottlenose dolphins. These dolphins prefer to live in pods and are very smart and social. They communicate with other dolphins through whistle noises, and they're active swimmers that can often be seen doing flips and leaps. They prefer tropical waters and can be found in the shallows of the Bahamas and along the southeastern and Gulf coasts of the United States.

# CLYMENE DOLPHIN
## STENELLA CLYMENE

**WHERE:** Atlantic Ocean
**LENGTH:** 5¾ feet (1¾ meters)
**LOOK FOR:** Streamlined body with a tricolor pattern
**DOLPHIN DATA:** This species of dolphin is incredibly special because it is the only recognized hybrid species of dolphin, which means that the whole species was descended from breeding between two different types of dolphins: the striped dolphin (see page 32) and the spinner dolphin (see page 47). Clymene dolphins often have a shorter beak than spinner dolphins, as well as distinctive dark marks on their face around their eyes and lips.

44

In ancient Greek myths, common bottlenose dolphins were said to save men from drowning or shark attacks, and although there are no modern reports of dolphins saving people, they have been known to help other dolphins in their pods get to the surface if they're injured or having trouble breathing.

# COMMON BOTTLENOSE DOLPHIN
## TURSIOPS TRUNCATUS

**WHERE:** Tropical Atlantic and Pacific Oceans
**LENGTH:** 6½ to 13 feet (2 to 4 meters)
**LOOK FOR:** Dark gray back and paler underside with a short, stubby snout
**DOLPHIN DATA:** When you picture a dolphin, you're likely thinking of something like the common bottlenose dolphin. The common bottlenose is considered to be the most well-known type of dolphin, and it is the largest species of beaked dolphin. These popular dolphins are well known for their tricks, and they're able to do acrobatics, locate hidden objects, and play with balls.

Although it's rare, common bottlenose dolphins are one of the few types of dolphins that will breed with other species, and scientists have studied cases where common bottlenose dolphins and short-beaked common dolphins (see page 37) had a calf together.

# SPINNER DOLPHIN
## STENELLA LONGIROSTRIS

**WHERE:** Tropical oceans around the world
**LENGTH:** 5 to 6½ feet (1½ to 2 meters)
**LOOK FOR:** Pale underbelly, light gray on the sides, and dark gray on the back
**DOLPHIN DATA:** These acrobatic dolphins are often seen leaping out of the water and twisting in the air in a spinning motion, which is how they got their nickname. They prefer to live in groups in warm waters and are often found in shallow areas by the coast, as well as in oceans all over the world. These small, slim dolphins are mostly gray with a few white patches and long beaks. There are a few subspecies of spinner dolphins, and this type of dolphin is thought to have mated with the striped dolphin (see page 32) to create a hybrid species, the Clymene dolphin (see page 44).

*There are actually three distinct types of spinner dolphins on this page! The left two are called* Stenella longirostris longirostris, *while the right two are* Stenella longirostris orientalis. *The center dolphin is a hybrid of the two, which you can tell by its unique coloration.*

Rough-toothed dolphins communicate with other members of their species using clicking and whistling noises, and they use echolocation to help them navigate, where they make a noise and then use the echo to understand their surroundings.

# ROUGH-TOOTHED DOLPHIN

## STENO BREDANENSIS

**WHERE:** Tropical oceans around the world
**LENGTH:** 6½ to 8 feet (2 to 2½ meters)
**LOOK FOR:** White, uneven splotches and rough, ridged teeth
**DOLPHIN DATA:** These dolphins would go through a lot of toothbrushes! Their teeth have rough ridges along them that are so noticeable they gave these dolphins their name. Although they have been seen both along the coast and offshore, they seem to prefer the deeper waters of the open ocean. These grayish dolphins have sloped foreheads that give their head a cone shape. They're fast swimmers and often swim just below the surface so that their dorsal fins are visible from above. They often travel in pods and will swim along with other whales and dolphins.

48

# INDO-PACIFIC BOTTLENOSE DOLPHIN

## TURSIOPS ADUNCUS

**WHERE:** Indian Ocean and Pacific Ocean

**LENGTH:** 8 feet (2½ meters)

**LOOK FOR:** Nearly identical to common bottlenose dolphins (see page 45), but with a longer beak

**DOLPHIN DATA:** The idea of living with a parasite doesn't sound like a lot of fun, but Indo-Pacific bottlenose dolphins don't mind parasites at all! In fact, these dolphins often act as hosts for parasites in what's known as a symbiotic relationship, where both the dolphins and the parasites benefit from each other.

This bottlenose dolphin is very closely related to the common bottlenose dolphin, but the Indo-Pacific bottlenose is usually smaller than the common bottlenose. These dolphins can live for an incredibly long time, and the oldest known Indo-Pacific bottlenose dolphin in the wild is a 49-year-old female. Like the common bottlenose dolphin, these dolphins are very social, and they'll sometimes form pods that include common bottlenose dolphins or even Indo-Pacific humpback dolphins (see page 43).

*Indo-Pacific bottlenose dolphins are sometimes seen picking up sponges off the seafloor, but scientists aren't sure whether this is another type of symbiotic relationship or just a way that the dolphins play.*

# ATLANTIC WHITE-SIDED DOLPHIN

## LAGENORHYNCHUS ACUTUS

**WHERE:** North Atlantic Ocean

**LENGTH:** 8 to 9¾ feet (2½ to 3 meters)

**LOOK FOR:** A distinct white or yellow stripe along the side

**DOLPHIN DATA:** Have you ever gone on a road trip with your whole family? Atlantic white-sided dolphins (left) travel in pods of hundreds, and the calves (young dolphins) will travel alongside their mothers. The Atlantic white-sided dolphin prefers cool, deep northern waters, especially along the coasts of Newfoundland and Massachusetts.

# WHITE-BEAKED DOLPHIN

## LAGENORHYNCHUS ALBIROSTRIS

**WHERE:** North Atlantic Ocean

**LENGTH:** 6½ to 9¾ feet (2 to 3 meters)

**LOOK FOR:** Light gray coloration with distinct white stripes along back of body

**DOLPHIN DATA:** You might have already guessed, but the white-beaked dolphin (second from left) gets its name from its white beak. These dolphins prefer to live in groups in cool, deep water, especially around Greenland, Iceland, and Europe, but they migrate as far south as Cape Cod, Massachusetts, in the winter.

*The white-beaked dolphin is a short-beaked dolphin that's mostly gray with some patches of lighter coloring, which can make them look a little like the Atlantic white-sided dolphin (above), but the white-beaked dolphin does not have a yellow stripe like the Atlantic white-sided dolphin.*

Pacific white-sided dolphins are active and social and are often seen near the surface of the water. Sometimes they'll perform tricks like jumping out of the water and doing somersaults. The unique color pattern on the lower dolphin is known as a Brownell form, after Dr. Robert L. Brownell Jr., a prominent marine biologist.

# PACIFIC WHITE-SIDED DOLPHIN

## LAGENORHYNCHUS OBLIQUIDENS

**WHERE:** North Pacific Ocean

**LENGTH:** 6½ to 8 feet (2 to 2½ meters)

**LOOK FOR:** A long, curved dorsal fin and off-white patches on the sides of the body

**DOLPHIN DATA:** Wondering what the difference is between the Atlantic white-sided dolphin (far left) and the Pacific white-sided dolphin? They're similar species, but the biggest difference is where they live. Pacific white-sided dolphins typically live in the cool, deep waters of the northern Pacific Ocean, where they can dive down more than 3,000 feet (914 meters) underwater. Pacific white-sided dolphins have dark gray, light gray, and white color patterns, and they have a large, hooked dorsal fin.

# BIG MELONS & SQUARE FACES

## HARBOR PORPOISE
### PHOCOENA PHOCOENA

**WHERE:** Northern Hemisphere, especially in cold waters
**LENGTH:** 5 to 6½ feet (1½ to 2 meters)
**LOOK FOR:** Small, rounded head and dark chin with body speckles
**PORPOISE PROFILE:** This porpoise's name tells you exactly where to find it. It prefers harbor-like areas, such as bays, estuaries, and river mouths, and it can survive in both freshwater and saltwater. These dolphins swim near the surface of the water and are frequently spotted by whale watchers, but they don't usually interact with boats and aren't often seen jumping out of the water.

For cetaceans, a melon is more than just a head. Toothed whales and dolphins have a mass on their forehead called a melon, and this organ helps them with communication and echolocation, where they use sounds and echoes to navigate.

Heads are important in identifying different species, from their shape to their markings. Here, we look at some of the most interesting and unique heads around.

# BURMEISTER'S PORPOISE

## PHOCOENA SPINIPINNIS

**WHERE:** South America
**LENGTH:** 5 feet (1½ meters)
**LOOK FOR:** Smooth, flat forehead and dark patches around the eyes
**PORPOISE PROFILE:** Don't expect to see a Burmeister's porpoise in the wild. This porpoise is very shy and will swim away from approaching boats or people. The Burmeister's porpoise was named for the scientist who first described the species in the 1800s. This dark gray porpoise prefers coastal, shallow waters and is sometimes seen along river estuaries. It has small, unique ridges along its dorsal fin called tubercles.

*Before they were seen in the wild, a dead Burmeister's porpoise was found on a beach and nicknamed the black porpoise, because its skin appeared to be black. Scientists now know that these porpoises are not naturally black, but they do turn from dark gray to black within a few minutes of dying.*

Long-finned pilot whales display some interesting, and entertaining, behaviors. They like to lift their tails out of the water and then hit them down to make a slapping noise, and they will stick their heads straight up out of the water, look around along the surface, and then drop back underwater in a move called spyhopping.

# LONG-FINNED PILOT WHALE

## GLOBICEPHALA MELAS

**WHERE:** Worldwide in cold water, especially near the Arctic and Antarctic
**LENGTH:** 14¾ to 19¾ feet (4½ to 6 meters)
**LOOK FOR:** Two, long, crescent-shaped pectoral flippers and a white anchor shape on their underside
**DOLPHIN DATA:** You might think of airplanes when you hear the word *pilot*, and you're not that far off. Pilots in the air help planes filled with people navigate. In pods of pilot whales, there's usually one leader, or pilot, in the pod that takes charge. These whales have very long fins, although there is also the short-finned pilot whale (see page 59), but the one part of their name that's not correct is the term "whale." Although they're large, they're technically a type of dolphin.

# SOUTHERN BOTTLENOSE WHALE

## HYPEROODON PLANIFRONS

**WHERE:** Southern Hemisphere
**LENGTH:** 24½ feet (7½ meters)
**LOOK FOR:** Large, prominent forehead and small snout
**WHALE WATCH:** Southern bottlenose whales don't like to get too cold, so in the winters they migrate to warm, tropical waters. Then, in the summer, they travel back to the cool Antarctic waters. These gray-brown whales are very closely related to northern bottlenose whales (see page 60). They prefer to live deep at sea and will often dive under the water for up to 45 minutes.

# SHORT-FINNED PILOT WHALE

## GLOBICEPHALA MACRORHYNCHUS

**WHERE:** Atlantic Ocean, Pacific Ocean, and Indian Ocean

**LENGTH:** 13 to 19¾ feet (4 to 6 meters)

**LOOK FOR:** Long, curved flippers and a lighter patch on the back of the dorsal fin

**WHALE WATCH:** You'll need to stay up very late to spot short-finned pilot whales in the wild. They're nocturnal, so they're much more active at night than during the day. Like its relative, the long-finned pilot whale (see page 56), this whale is actually part of the dolphin family. Short-finned pilot whales prefer to live in deep, warm water. They travel mostly in pods and they don't seem to stay in one place for very long. Scientists think they likely follow their prey, which is mostly squid, octopus, and some small fish.

# NORTHERN BOTTLENOSE WHALE
## HYPEROODON AMPULLATUS

**WHERE:** North Atlantic

**LENGTH:** 32 feet (9¾ meters)

**LOOK FOR:** Blunt head, small snout, and chocolate, olive brown, and gray colorations

**WHALE WATCH:** Have you ever tried to touch the bottom of a pool? It might feel like a long way down, but that distance would be no problem to northern bottlenose whales. These strong divers can stay underwater for more than an hour and reach depths of about 4,700 feet (1,432 meters). They usually dive to catch squid and fish.

Like southern bottlenose whales (see page 57), northern bottlenose whales are beaked whales that prefer cold, deep water and are more brown than gray. They travel in groups and will migrate to warmer waters in the winter.

# RISSO'S DOLPHIN
## GRAMPUS GRISEUS

**WHERE:** Worldwide

**LENGTH:** 9¾ to 13 feet (3 to 4 meters)

**LOOK FOR:** Blunt head and a gray or olive brown body that turns white with age

**DOLPHIN DATA:** Did you know dolphins can have cliques? Like a lot of other dolphins, Risso's dolphins form pods, but what's unusual about Risso's dolphins is that they don't make random groups. Instead, they pick members of their pods based on age or sex, which gives them a social structure that's more like people than most other dolphins. Risso's dolphins prefer a habitat with a steep slope, such as along a continental shelf, but they are found all over the world.

*Risso's dolphins (center) often have large, white scars on their bodies, and they get more scars as they get older. The scars are caused by attacks from other animals or from hunting for their prey, which is mainly squid and octopus. Scientists think that these dolphins are slower healers than other types of marine mammals, making the scars more apparent.*

# INDO-PACIFIC FINLESS PORPOISE
## NEOPHOCAENA PHOCAENOIDES

**WHERE:** Indian and western Pacific Oceans

**LENGTH:** 5 feet (1½ meters)

**LOOK FOR:** Lack of a dorsal fin, with a back ridge that appears to be covered in warts

**PORPOISE PROFILE:** What do you call a porpoise without a dorsal fin? A finless porpoise, of course! These small porpoises can live in both freshwater and saltwater, and have been seen in shallow coastal waters and in rivers like the Yangtze in China. They have dark gray skin with blue patches, and their skin seems to turn darker as they age. These porpoises are slow swimmers and very rarely jump out of the water, although they do roll to the side when they surface to breathe.

# EAST ASIAN FINLESS PORPOISE
## NEOPHOCAENA ASIAORIENTALIS SUNAMERI

**WHERE:** Coast along mainland China, the Penghu Islands, and coastal Vietnam

**LENGTH:** 6½ feet (2 meters)

**LOOK FOR:** Rounded head and a long ridge running down the back in place of a dorsal fin

**PORPOISE PROFILE:** These perpetually smiling cetaceans were only recently defined as a separate subspecies from their cousin, the Indo-Pacific finless porpoise (left). They like to make their home in shallow waters along coasts and estuaries, making them especially susceptible to injury by boats in harbors. They are also heavily impacted by water pollution, as well as habitat loss from expanding harbors and shipping lines. Although there isn't an exact number of how many are left in the wild, some scientists estimate they have had an almost 70 percent population decline from the late 1970s to the early 2000s.

# AUSTRALIAN SNUBFIN DOLPHIN

## ORCAELLA HEINSOHNI

**WHERE:** Australia

**LENGTH:** 6½ to 7⅓ feet (2 to 2¼ meters)

**LOOK FOR:** Soft, rounded head and dark coloration that grows light with age

**DOLPHIN DATA:** This dolphin looks a lot like the Irrawaddy River dolphin (see page 23), but it has more colors on its skin than the Irrawaddy. Australian snubfin dolphins are gray with patches of blue and white, and they're found in shallow waters near the coast of northern Australia, especially near river mouths and in areas with sea grass and coral.

# SPERM WHALE

## PHYSETER MACROCEPHALUS

**WHERE:** Worldwide

**LENGTH:** 39⅓ to 52½ feet (12 to 16 meters)

**LOOK FOR:** Square-shaped head and a small dorsal fin set back on the body

**WHALE WATCH:** Have you ever heard of a whale called Moby Dick? He's not a real whale, but he is a famous fictional whale from a book of the same name by Herman Melville, and he was well known for his massive head and body. The description certainly makes sense—sperm whales are very easy to identify with their large, square heads. The shape comes from the large organ on the front of a sperm whale's head that holds up to 500 gallons of a waxlike, oily substance called spermaceti. This organ is thought to help sperm whales with echolocation, and some scientists think that the substance may also help the whales to adjust their buoyancy, so that they can dive more efficiently.

Sperm whales are found in every ocean and prefer deep, ice-free waters. These whales can dive deep under the water and remain below the surface for more than an hour at a time. These whales were once intensely hunted because of their large size and valuable spermaceti, but restrictions on hunting have helped the population to grow again.

*Male sperm whales are significantly larger than females and can get as large as 65½ feet (20 meters) long.*

# DWARF SPERM WHALE

## KOGIA SIMA

**WHERE:** Worldwide in tropical waters
**LENGTH:** 6½ to 8 feet (2 to 2½ meters)
**LOOK FOR:** Slightly pointed snout with a conical head and an askew blowhole
**WHALE WATCH:** If you watch a dwarf sperm whale dive, you might think it's sinking. Instead of diving headfirst, dwarf sperm whales slowly sink down into the water before they dive, but once they go under, they can dive deep down into the ocean.

Like the related pygmy sperm whale (below), the dwarf sperm whale is rare in the wild, and it's often difficult to tell which species is which because they are so physically similar. The main difference is the position of the dorsal fin; dwarf sperm whales have fins that are mostly in the center of their backs, whereas pygmy sperm whales have dorsal fins that are farther back on their bodies.

# PYGMY SPERM WHALE

## KOGIA BREVICEPS

**WHERE:** Worldwide in tropical waters
**LENGTH:** 9¾ feet (3 meters)
**LOOK FOR:** A single, askew blowhole and a pale underbelly that fades into gray
**WHALE WATCH:** Look, a shark! Just kidding, the pygmy sperm whale is actually a whale, but it has a large, blunt head that makes it look a little like a shark, and it has white markings around the face that resemble gills. Don't expect to see an active pygmy sperm whale. They move slowly and quietly, and they'll often float motionlessly at the surface of the water. Pygmy sperm whales prefer warm, tropical waters, but they are not often seen at sea. They are closely related to the sperm whale (left), although they're much smaller in size. They eat mostly squid, fish, shrimp, and crabs, and seem to prefer deep water to hunt for food.

*Like pygmy sperm whales, dwarf sperm whales have white markings on their faces in the same spot where a shark would have gills.*

# BEAKED WHALE BONANZA

**B**eaked whales are a type of toothed whale that has a pronounced, snout-like beak rather than a flat or square face, and these types of whales are well known for being good divers. The beak gives them an appearance similar to dolphins. They prefer to be deep under the water, which makes them difficult to study and understand. Here, we look at different species of this unique type of whale.

## TRUE'S BEAKED WHALE
### MESOPLODON MIRUS

**WHERE:** Atlantic and Indian Oceans

**LENGTH:** 17¼ feet (5¼ meters)

**LOOK FOR:** Bluish gray body and two small teeth that protrude from the lower jaw

**WHALE WATCH:** Smile for the camera! In 2017, these interesting whales were captured on underwater cameras, which was helpful for scientists to provide a good description of them. There is currently only one species of True's beaked whale, but because there are two different populations, one in the Northern Hemisphere and one in the Southern Hemisphere, scientists wonder whether there may be two subspecies of this type of whale.

# SOWERBY'S BEAKED WHALE

## *MESOPLODON BIDENS*

**WHERE:** North Atlantic Ocean

**LENGTH:** 16½ feet (5 meters)

**LOOK FOR:** Slender, spindle-shaped body, a dark olive to gray-brown head, and a white belly

**WHALE WATCH:** Sowerby's beaked whale was one of the first beaked whales discovered and was described as early as 1804, but scientists still don't know much about it because it prefers to live in cold, deep waters and isn't seen often. It has two prominent teeth on its lower jaw and can dive under the water for about 30 minutes. These whales are gray, brown, or greenish in color with lighter bellies, and they sometimes have scars on their bodies.

# GERVAIS' BEAKED WHALE

## *MESOPLODON EUROPAEUS*

**WHERE:** Atlantic Ocean

**LENGTH:** 13 to 16½ feet (4 to 5 meters)

**LOOK FOR:** Spindle-shaped body and small, sharklike dorsal fin

**WHALE WATCH:** Although Gervais' beaked whales have some scars on their body, they don't seem to have as many as other species of beaked whales. These dark gray whales tend to become darker as they age. They seem to prefer warm, tropical waters, but they're not often seen. They travel in small groups and suction feed on squid, fish, and shrimp.

# ARNOUX'S BEAKED WHALE

## BERARDIUS ARNUXII

**WHERE:** Southern Hemisphere

**LENGTH:** 26¼ to 39⅓ feet (8 to 12 meters)

**LOOK FOR:** Large, protruding forehead and long snout with two sets of front teeth in the lower jaw

**WHALE WATCH:** These grandfatherly whales can live up to 84 years, and as they get older, they usually develop scars on their skin. Arnoux's beaked whales prefer the open ocean and cold waters around the Antarctic, but they have sometimes been spotted in shallow coastal waters.

# KARASU WHALE

## BERARDIUS MINIMUS

**WHERE:** North Pacific Ocean

**LENGTH:** Estimated 23 feet (7 meters)

**LOOK FOR:** Small, hooked dorsal fin and a black to gray coloration

**WHALE WATCH:** Have you ever seen a raven in the ocean before? If you speak Japanese, then you might already know that *karasu* is Japanese for "raven." The karasu whale (top) was first discovered off the coast of Japan in 2016, and scientists aren't sure whether this whale should be its own species or whether it's really a Baird's beaked whale (bottom). Because this whale is smaller and darker than most Baird's beaked whales, scientists think it may be its own species.

# BAIRD'S BEAKED WHALE

## BERARDIUS BAIRDII

**WHERE:** North Pacific Ocean

**LENGTH:** 32¾ to 36 feet (10 to 11 meters)

**LOOK FOR:** Dense, protruding foreheads that turn from brownish gray to white as they age and a noticeable underbite

**WHALE WATCH:** Imagine not having any teeth on top of your mouth These whales have two pairs of teeth, both on their bottom jaw. Baird's beaked whale (right) is the northern relative of Arnoux's beaked whale (left); the two are very similar in appearance, and the only major difference between the two species is where they live. Baird's whales live in a very limited part of the Pacific Ocean in cold, deep water. Like their southern relatives, they have gray bodies that are often marked by white scars.

# ANDREWS' BEAKED WHALE

## MESOPLODON BOWDOINI

**WHERE:** Indian and Pacific Oceans

**LENGTH:** 14¾ to 16½ feet (4½ to 5 meters)

**LOOK FOR:** Short beak with arched mouth line and a pale markings around the mouth

**WHALE WATCH:** Andrews' whales (top left) prefer cool, deep waters around Australia and New Zealand, and it is rare to see these whales in the wild because they spend very little time near the surface. Andrews' whales are dark gray in color, but their beaks are white. Most of what scientists know about this species comes from deceased whales that have washed up on the shore.

# GRAY'S BEAKED WHALE

## MESOPLODON GRAYI

**WHERE:** Southern Hemisphere

**LENGTH:** 16½ to 19¾ feet (5 to 6 meters)

**LOOK FOR:** Long, slender, white beak

**WHALE WATCH:** Gray's beaked whales (bottom left) typically live in deep water, but they have been occasionally been spotted in shallow waters and has even been found beached in New Zealand. Gray's whale pods have been spotted all over the Southern Hemisphere, and they typically travel in groups of 4 to 10. These whales have brown or gray bodies with a light or white beak. They sometimes have white spots on their bodies as well as scars.

# SHEPHERD'S BEAKED WHALE

## TASMACETUS SHEPHERDI

**WHERE:** Southern Hemisphere

**LENGTH:** 19½ to 23 feet (6 to 7 meters)

**LOOK FOR:** Gray-brown coloration with white or cream stomach and a white marking on the melon

**WHALE WATCH:** The Shepherd's beaked whale (top) is still a mystery. Scientists aren't sure exactly where this whale lives because there have only been four recorded sightings of this species at sea. Most beaked whales only have a few teeth on one jaw, but Shepherd's beaked whales have a full set of teeth on both their top and bottom jaw, and they eat both fish and squid.

# HECTOR'S BEAKED WHALE

## MESOPLODON HECTORI

**WHERE:** Southern Hemisphere

**LENGTH:** 13 feet (4 meters)

**LOOK FOR:** Dark patches around the eyes and a short, well-defined beak with white or gray coloration

**WHALE WATCH:** Can you imagine swallowing all your food whole? Male Hector's beaked whales only have one pair of teeth on their lower jaw, so scientists think they're suction feeders, which means that they eat fish or squid by sucking prey into their mouth using strong muscles and swallowing it whole, kind of like using a straw. Hector's beaked whales prefer to live in colder waters, and it's rare to see them in the wild. They are typically dark gray or brown, and they have scars on their bodies like many other beaked whales.

*Female Hector's beaked whales have darker faces with a white ring around them (above top), while males have white faces and a dark body (below bottom).*

# DERANIYAGALA'S BEAKED WHALE
## MESOPLODON HOTAULA

**WHERE:** Indian and South Pacific Oceans
**LENGTH:** 14¾ feet (4½ meters)
**LOOK FOR:** Gray-blue coloration
**WHALE WATCH:** Scientists have only been able to study this incredibly rare whale (left) fewer than 10 times. This gray-blue whale was originally discovered in 1963, and it has only been seen a handful of times since. Although scientists originally thought it might be the same species as the ginkgo-toothed beaked whale (see page 74), scientists eventually declared it a separate species and named it after the scientist who first discovered it.

# INDO-PACIFIC BEAKED WHALE

## INDOPACETUS PACIFICUS

**WHERE:** Eastern Pacific and Indian Ocean

**LENGTH:** 13 to 29½ feet (4 to 9 meters)

**LOOK FOR:** A large lower jaw that passes the upper jaw, with two small, oval-shaped teeth at the tip

**WHALE WATCH:** These deep-diving whales (center) can stay under the water for up to 45 minutes, which makes them rare to see in the ocean, but they have sometimes been spotted coming up out of the surface of the water (known as breaching). The Indo-Pacific beaked whale lives in deep water, and it has a dark gray or brown body marked with scars similar to many other species of beaked whales. When they have been seen in the wild, they're usually found in pods, and they sometimes associate with other species of marine mammals.

# SPADE-TOOTHED WHALE

## MESOPLODON TRAVERSII OR MESOPLODON BAHAMONDI

**WHERE:** New Zealand

**LENGTH:** Estimated 16½ feet (5 meters)

**LOOK FOR:** Two large tusks that curve over the upper snout in males

**WHALE WATCH:** Although most beaked whales are rare, the spade-toothed whale (right) is thought to be the rarest species of all. In fact, the spade-toothed whale has never been seen alive, so scientists can only guess at its behavior. The species was first recorded in the 1800s, but after years without a sighting it was suspected to be extinct. It wasn't seen again until the mid-1900s, and scientists have gone decades between sightings without any proof that this species still exists. The most recent sighting was in 2010, when two deceased whales washed up on a beach in New Zealand.

# GINKGO-TOOTHED BEAKED WHALE

## MESOPLODON GINKGODENS

**WHERE:** Pacific and Indian Oceans

**LENGTH:** 16½ feet (5 meters)

**LOOK FOR:** Small, pointed fins, a smooth forehead, and a long beak with largely covered lower teeth

**WHALE WATCH:** There's a type of leaf in China called a ginkgo leaf that has a fanlike shape, and these whales are named after the plant because their two bottom teeth look a lot like ginkgo leaves. Most of what scientists know about this whale is from beached, deceased whales, but they suspect that this deep-ocean dweller prefers warmer waters and likely eats fish and squid. These dark gray whales sometimes have white spots on their bodies, and ginkgo-toothed beaked whales have fewer scars than other species of beaked whale.

*Bite marks from cookiecutter sharks are often visible on beaked whales like ginkgo-toothed whales, and it's thought that the sharks attack them to take a bite out of the whale's nutrient-rich fat, although this doesn't kill the whales because the scars from the bites usually heal.*

# BLAINVILLE'S BEAKED WHALE

## MESOPLODON DENSIROSTRIS

**WHERE:** Worldwide in warm waters

**LENGTH:** 14¾ feet (4½ meters)

**LOOK FOR:** Steel blue to dark brown coloration that darkens as they age and pale spots across the body

**WHALE WATCH:** Male Blainville's beaked whales usually have lots of scars on their body, and scientists think they're from fights between males over female whales. They prefer deep water in warm or tropical areas, and they are one of the most well-studied types of beaked whale. These dark blue to brown whales have long, narrow bodies. They are able to dive deep under the water using echolocation to help them navigate, and they can stay under for more than 45 minutes. They are suction feeders who eat mostly squid, and the males have large, exposed teeth extending up from their lower jaw.

# HUBBS' BEAKED WHALE

## MESOPLODON CARLHUBBSI

**WHERE:** North Pacific Ocean

**LENGTH:** 16½ feet (5 meters)

**LOOK FOR:** Raised white forehead, white elongated beak, and two large tusks that protrude upward from the lower jaw

**WHALE WATCH:** It's very uncommon to see this whale (top) in the wild because it prefers deep water, but one was spotted off the coast of California in 1945. It was originally thought to be an Andrews' beaked whale (see page 70), but it was made into its own species years later. These whales are usually dark gray, and the males have a white patch along the tip of their beak and forehead. The males of this species have scars all over their bodies, and scientists believe they may be more competitive than other species of beaked whales.

# PYGMY BEAKED WHALE

## MESOPLODON PERUVIANUS

**WHERE:** Peru

**LENGTH:** 11½ (3½ meters)

**LOOK FOR:** Slender, spindle-shaped body with two teeth protruding from the lower jaw

**WHALE WATCH:** Male pygmy beaked whales (bottom) have a distinct pattern on their backs that has been described as a chevron shape, and these brown-gray whales have very thick tails. This species is the smallest of the beaked whales, and pygmy beaked whales have only been seen in the waters near Peru, although scientists believe they might live in a wider area.

# PERRIN'S BEAKED WHALE

## *MESOPLODON PERRINI*

**WHERE:** North Pacific Ocean

**LENGTH:** 14¾ feet (4½ meters)

**LOOK FOR:** Small, thick, gray body with a set of large triangular teeth that protrude from the lower jaw

**WHALE WATCH:** The Perrin's beaked whale (top) is one of the newest species of beaked whales and one of the most recently seen. Although it's only been seen fewer than 10 times, it was first discovered in 1975 and has been spotted as recently as May 2019. Perrin's beaked whale looks very similar to Hector's beaked whale (see page 71), and it can be almost impossible to tell the two apart at sea. These whales are often dark gray with lighter gray on the bellies and have occasional patches of white.

# STEJNEGER'S BEAKED WHALE

## *MESOPLODON STEJNEGERI*

**WHERE:** North Pacific Ocean

**LENGTH:** 16½ to 18 feet (5 to 5½ meters)

**LOOK FOR:** Relatively small head, with rounded teeth that protrude from the lower jaw in males that can restrict the upper jaw

**WHALE WATCH:** These dark gray whales (bottom) have a dark patch on their head that makes them look like they're wearing a helmet. It is very uncommon to see this species, like other beaked whales, in the wild, but scientists believe it lives in the cold, deep waters of the North Pacific and Bering Sea. They have two large, pointed teeth on their lower jaw. Stejneger's beaked whales have scars on their bodies like other beaked whales, leading scientists to believe they fight often.

# ENDANGERED CETACEANS

**M**any species of whales and dolphins have become endangered, which means that the International Union for Conservation of Nature (IUCN) has determined that the species faces a very high risk of extinction in the wild. Due to the natural order of the food chain, rare species sometimes become naturally endangered, but many times the threat to these animals comes from humans. Whales are naturally large predators and are often at the top of the food chain, but humans throughout history have hunted and killed them for profit, which led to large declines in their population. Although most of the intentional hunting activity has stopped, it can take decades for the species to recover, and some do not and become extinct. Fishing accidents are also a common problem, especially for smaller dolphins that are easily caught in nets by mistake, known as bycatch, injuring or killing them. Even beyond these accidents, pollution and climate change have a lasting impact on the habitat of these marine mammals, and the changes to their homes and food source can be too hard to overcome. Staying aware of the problems that these species face can help scientists and lawmakers better combat these threats.

# NORTH ATLANTIC RIGHT WHALE

## EUBALAENA GLACIALIS

**WHERE:** North Atlantic Ocean

**LENGTH:** 42½ to 59 feet (13 to 18 meters)

**LOOK FOR:** Large, mostly black whale with a paddle-shaped flippers and a large head

**WHALE WATCH:** Can you picture a traffic jam on the highway? Unfortunately for North Atlantic right whales, they live along a ship route that has a lot of traffic. Because of this, these slow-swimming whales are often injured by passing boats or caught in fishing nets. Although these baleen whales once had a large population, only about 424 are now left in existence. Years ago, whalers hunted North Atlantic right whales because of their slow speed and preference for being near land, leading to a steady population decline. Scientists have been watching them for years, but the number of whales that die each year is larger than the number born, which leads the scientists to believe it's only a matter of time before this whale is extinct.

# SEI WHALE
## BALAENOPTERA BOREALIS

**WHERE:** North Atlantic and North Pacific Oceans
**LENGTH:** 42½ to 49½ feet (13 to 15 meters)
**LOOK FOR:** A single ridge running from the nose to two blowholes
**WHALE WATCH:** The sei whale and its fishy best friend have matching names! In Norway, a type of fish called *seje* lives along the same pathway where the sei whale migrates. Because the two were spotted together so often, the whales were given the name *sei* to pair with the fish.

Sei whales became the target of aggressive whaling in the 19th and 20th centuries, leading to a sudden drop in their population. In recent years the population has started to increase again because of the whale's protected status, but it is still considered an endangered species.

*The sei whale is most often found in the open ocean and although they are not strong divers, they are very fast swimmers and are one of the quickest swimming whales.*

# NORTH PACIFIC RIGHT WHALE

## EUBALAENA JAPONICA

**WHERE:** North Pacific Ocean

**LENGTH:** 46 to 55¾ feet (14 to 17 meters)

**LOOK FOR:** Huge head with horned growths call callosities

**WHALE WATCH:** You might think lice are disgusting, but these largely black whales (top) don't seem to mind them. They have patches of rough, white skin called callosities that are sometimes home to barnacles or whale lice. While whale lice aren't the same kind humans get, their names are very similar!

This large whale has been the target of illegal hunting, and because its habitat is in the path of many major boating routes, it has been injured and killed in shipping collisions. This rare species is considered endangered, with just a few hundred left in the world.

Water that fin whales spout from their blowhole can reach 15 to 20 feet (4½ to 6 meters) high!

# FIN WHALE

## BALAENOPTERA PHYSALUS

**WHERE:** All major oceans and open seas

**LENGTH:** 69 to 78¾ feet (21 to 24 meters)

**LOOK FOR:** Dark markings on the left side of the snout, white markings on the right

**WHALE WATCH:** With unusual markings on their lips that are dark on the left side and white on the right, fin whales (top and bottom left) look like they're wearing costume makeup! Fin whales get their name from the small dorsal fin low on their backs. They're one of the largest whales that will swim with their fin exposed above the surface of the water, so they're easy to spot on the open ocean. These whales can live for 75 years or more in the wild, but because hunters in the early 1900s targeted them, their population quickly declined. These massive whales are incredibly fast swimmers, and although they seem to prefer cool, coastal polar waters, they have occasionally been spotted in tropical climates.

# MĀUI'S DOLPHIN

## CEPHALORHYNCHUS HECTORI MĀUI

**WHERE:** New Zealand
**LENGTH:** 3 to 5½ feet (1 to 1½ meters)
**LOOK FOR:** Small, darkly colored body with a rounded dorsal fin and white underbody
**DOLPHIN DATA:** Have you ever seen a car or a motorcycle with flames on the sides? These small dolphins are mostly white with distinctive markings on their bodies in a flame-like pattern. Although they're closely related to Hector's dolphins (right), Māui's dolphins are considered their own species and live only around the North Island of New Zealand.

Māui's dolphins are a critically endangered species, and some scientists estimate that fewer than 70 adult Māui's dolphins are left. These dolphins are very vulnerable to being caught in fishing nets, especially particular nets called gill nets, and death from fishing net injuries is likely the largest factor in the population's decline.

*Māui's dolphins are incredibly playful, and they'll jump and play with other members of their pods. They've also been seen blowing bubbles and playing with seaweed.*

# HECTOR'S DOLPHIN

## CEPHALORHYNCHUS HECTORI

**WHERE:** New Zealand

**LENGTH:** 5 feet (1½ meters)

**LOOK FOR:** Small, spindle-shaped, dark gray body with a pale gray stomach

**DOLPHIN DATA:** Do you live far away from your cousins? These small dolphins live only around the South Island of New Zealand in shallow water and are not able to swim in deep open waters, keeping them separate from the related Māui's dolphins (left) that live around New Zealand's North Island. Hector's dolphins are very small, pale gray dolphins that are named for Sir James Hector, the first person to examine a dolphin of this species. They often form small pods and feed on fish on the ocean surface or seafloor.

These dolphins are an endangered species because they are often accidentally caught and injured or killed in fishing nets. Younger dolphins are more likely to be caught, leading scientists to believe that they may start to learn to avoid the nets as they age.

# YANGTZE FINLESS PORPOISE

## NEOPHOCAENA ASIAEORIENTALIS

**WHERE:** Yangtze River

**LENGTH:** 5 to 6½ feet (1½ to 2 meters)

**LOOK FOR:** Rounded head and long, light gray body

**PORPOISE PROFILE:** Sometimes places pass laws to help protect endangered species. In China, it's illegal to harm a finless porpoise (top), and special areas of the Yangtze River are protected areas where people aren't allowed to visit. This helps the number of these porpoises grow. Located only in the Yangtze River of China, the Yangtze finless porpoise gets its name because it doesn't have a dorsal fin. This critically endangered freshwater porpoise has mostly been harmed by human causes. Fishing and boating accidents have killed some of the population, while man-made changes to the river have limited their food supply.

# BAIJI

## LIPOTES VEXILLIFER

**WHERE:** Yangtze River

**LENGTH:** 5 to 6½ feet (1½ to 2 meters)

**LOOK FOR:** Rounded body with a long, thin snout

**DOLPHIN DATA:** Are you a fan of dinosaurs? Although dinosaurs went extinct a long time ago, other species of animals can still go extinct today. The baiji (bottom) hasn't been seen in years, so scientists think it may already be an extinct species, and those who have seen it are very lucky. It's considered critically endangered, and if any are left in the wild, scientists suspect that the number is fewer than 100.

This freshwater dolphin is found only in the Yangtze River in China and prefers to live in areas next to sandbars. Because the river is turbulent and murky, seeing isn't very useful for these dolphins, so they navigate mostly by sound.

# SOUTH ASIAN RIVER DOLPHIN
## PLATANISTA GANGETICA

**WHERE:** Ganges River

**LENGTH:** 6½ to 8 feet (2 to 2½ meters)

**LOOK FOR:** Grayish brown to pink coloration with small, nearly invisible eyes and a long, slender snout

**DOLPHIN DATA:** When you look in the mirror, you probably see your eyes right away, but you'd have trouble spotting a South Asian river dolphin's eyes! South Asian river dolphins are nicknamed "blind river dolphins" because they have very limited eyesight. Lucky for them, good eyesight wouldn't be very helpful to navigate in the dark, swirly waters of the river, and they can rely on other senses. These freshwater dolphins exist only in the rivers of southern Asia, and although there used to be two subspecies, these dolphins are now all considered to be one species. They have long flippers and teeth, and are gray, brown, or pink in color.

*Human changes to the rivers they live in have damaged the South Asian river dolphin's habitat, and rising pollution levels are a big threat. Populations of this endangered species are often cut off from one another by man-made dams, making it difficult for these dolphins to find mates.*

# SUPERLATIVE CETACEANS

**Y**ou might assume that all marine mammals are large and slow, and even though that's true for some, marine mammals come in all shapes, sizes, and speeds. There are porpoises that can swim as fast as a boat, whales that can sing, and even whales that can dive underwater for more than an hour. Here, we've gathered the best of the best among whales, dolphins, and porpoises to show you just how fantastic the world of marine mammals can be!

LONGEST LIFE

# BOWHEAD WHALE
## *BALAENA MYSTICETUS*

**WHERE:** Northern Hemisphere
**LENGTH:** 46 to 59 feet (14 to 18 meters)
**LOOK FOR:** Arched upper jaw shaped like an archer's bow
**WHALE WATCH:** This elderly whale has the distinction of being the longest-living whale, and in fact this species is one of the longest-living mammals on land or sea. This baleen whale, which prefers colder waters near the Arctic, has been estimated to live for more than 200 years! Scientists were able to estimate how old these whales can get by examining their eyes, and in some instances, they even found ivory and stone harpoon heads embedded in these whales' tough skin that led them to believe the bowhead whale could live for two full centuries.

Despite their long life span, these whales were once highly sought after by hunters, leading to them becoming endangered.

93

# BELUGA

## DELPHINAPTERUS LEUCAS

**WHERE:** Northern Hemisphere

**LENGTH:** 18 feet (5½ meters)

**LOOK FOR:** Large forehead, small snout, wide fins, and white coloration

**WHALE WATCH:** Sometimes called the white whale, adult belugas are the only whales that are fully white in color. They typically live in shallow coastal waters of Arctic areas, including the coasts along Canada, Iceland, Greenland, Norway, and Russia. They have large, rounded heads and use high-pitched calls to communicate.

You may have heard the song about baby belugas in the deep blue sea, and that's because the calves of these whales are well known for being incredibly adorable. Beluga calves are gray colored and measure in at about 5 feet (1½ meters) long when they're born. The newborns will swim alongside their mother and nurse from them for the first year of their life. Rarely, hybrid species have been documented when beluga whales mate with narwhals (right).

WHITEST WHALE

Narwhals are related to beluga whales and have mostly white bodies with brown and gray markings. They prefer cold Arctic waters around Greenland, Canada, and Russia, and are very rarely seen in the wild.

LARGEST TOOTH

# NARWHAL
## MONODON MONOCEROS

**WHERE:** Arctic waters
**LENGTH:** 13 to 18 feet (4 to 5½ meters)
**LOOK FOR:** Long, hornlike tooth
**WHALE WATCH:** The long tusk growing out of a narwhal's head may look like a horn, but don't be fooled. That tusk is actually an extremely long tooth. In fact, narwhals only have two teeth, and in females those teeth stay a normal size. But in males, the left tooth grows straight through the whale's upper lip and extends out in front of it in a tusk that can be almost as long as the rest of its body. The tusk has nerve endings that can feel along the ocean floor, and although it will sometimes break, it typically grows back.

# HUMPBACK WHALE

## MEGAPTERA NOVAEANGLIAE

BEST SINGER

**WHERE:** All major oceans

**LENGTH:** 39½ to 49 feet (12 to 15 meters)

**LOOK FOR:** Huge head and tail, with knob-like tubercles on the head

**WHALE WATCH:** If you've seen the movie *Finding Nemo*, you might remember Dory's attempts to "speak whale." She might have been onto something, because humpback whales are very vocal. Male humpbacks are known for their singing abilities, and they have a wide range of "songs" that they use to communicate. The songs are made up of many sounds and can differ from one season to the next.

Humpback whales, which are named for the humplike shape of their dorsal fin, migrate between polar and tropical waters, making them common to many different parts of the world. Although they were targets of hunting in the past, their population has been increasing in recent years.

*Humpback whales have a very interesting way of feeding in groups. When the group finds a school of prey, they swim around it in a circle, blowing bubbles with their mouths to make a ring around the school, sometimes called a bubble net. Then they swim up through the "net," encircling the school with their mouths wide open, catching any prey in their path.*

96

# BLUE WHALE
## BALAENOPTERA MUSCULUS

**WHERE:** Global
**LENGTH:** 98½ feet (30 meters)
**LOOK FOR:** Long, streamlined body and a U-shaped mouth
**WHALE WATCH:** The blue whale is a baleen whale that gets its name from its blue-gray color, but its real distinguishing feature is its size. This massive creature is the largest ocean mammal, growing to be nearly 100 feet (30 meters) long and weighing 200 tons (181½ metric tons). Even newborn blue whale calves can be up to 25 feet (7½ meters) long and weigh 3 tons (2¾ metric tons). Blue whales are found all over the world, in both tropical and polar waters, and they are thought to live for around 80 to 90 years in the wild. Like other baleen whales, they mainly eat krill, and because of their size, they don't have many natural predators.

BIGGEST

# GRAY WHALE
## *ESCHRICHTIUS ROBUSTUS*

**WHERE:** Pacific Ocean

**LENGTH:** 46 to 49 feet (14 to 15 meters)

**LOOK FOR:** Marbled gray color with small, narrow head and paddle-shaped flippers

**WHALE WATCH:** What's the longest trip you've ever taken? Every year, gray whales make a round-trip journey of nearly 13,000 miles (20,921 kilometers)! In October, they begin a two- to three-month journey from the cold polar waters of the Bering Sea to the warm waters near Mexico and southern California, covering up to 6,800 miles (10,943 kilometers) over the course of their journey south. Then, around March, they reverse the journey and travel back north for the summer. Newborn calves and their mothers will stay south longer, sometimes remaining into May, before returning north. Gray whales were named for their color and live primarily in the Pacific Ocean, although one or two have been seen in the Atlantic Ocean.

# VAQUITA
## *PHOCOENA SINUS*

**WHERE:** Gulf of California

**LENGTH:** 4 feet (1¼ meters)

**LOOK FOR:** Small, gray body with white underbelly and tiny snout with black coloration

**PORPOISE PROFILE:** This tiny porpoise, whose name means "little cow" in Spanish, almost never grows beyond 4 to 4½ feet (about 1½ meters) in length. That's smaller than most adult humans! Although this adorable porpoise may look cute, its small size makes it prone to accidentally being caught and killed in fishing nets. In fact, the vaquita is considered to be a critically endangered porpoise, and scientists estimate that there are fewer than 30 of them left alive. Although lawmakers in Mexico put a ban on the gill nets that often trap vaquitas, there are still many things that need to happen for the vaquitas to survive, including protecting their natural habitat. The small population exists only along the Gulf of California in Mexico, and they frequent shallow lagoons and murky shorelines.

SMALLEST

# KILLER WHALE
## ORCINUS ORCA

**WHERE:** Global
**LENGTH:** 23 to 26 feet (7 to 8 meters)
**LOOK FOR:** Black body with white patch behind eyes, on the flank, and underside of body
**DOLPHIN DATA:** Despite the name, killer whales aren't as dangerous as they might seem. These fierce predators with distinctive black-and-white markings prey on fish, squid, penguins, and sea lions. They don't naturally attack humans, so unless you get in the way of them and their prey, they won't harm you in the wild. These whales don't like to be kept captive, and there have been reports of them injuring staff members at aquatic parks. You might even remember seeing a famous orca named Willy trying to make his way from an aquatic park back to the ocean in the movie *Free Willy*.

Like other marine mammals, killer whales travel in pods, but the social structure in these groups is much more complex than other marine mammals. They coordinate their activities, and older members of the group are known for teaching the younger members of the group skills like hunting and parenting. Killer whales are found in oceans all over the world, but there are two distinct populations: one in the Northern Hemisphere and one in the Southern Hemisphere. The populations are not technically separate species, but they can look and act differently based on where they're found, to the point where the recently discovered type D killer whale (far right) may not even be the same species!

SMARTEST

*Killer whales are technically large dolphins rather than whales and are sometimes called orcas.*